D0773461

ONE DIRECTION
THE ULTIMATE FAN BOOK

Sarah-Louise James

TO KEEP YOU UP ALL NIGHT!

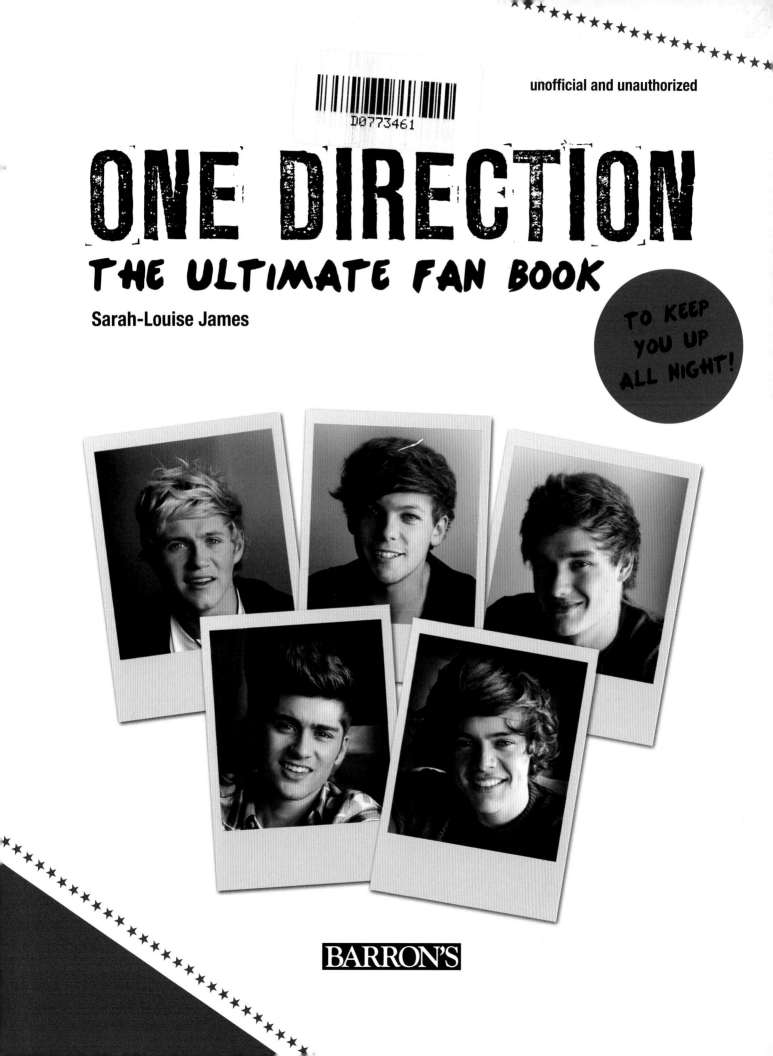

BARRON'S

INTRODUCTION

What has ten legs, masses of hair, and whose appearance causes ear-splitting screams? Answer: One Direction. And like a scary creature fitting the same description, more often than not, their sheer existence results in mass hysteria. But that's where the similarities end. 1D are much friendlier and way, way cuter! They are Louis Tomlinson, Zayn Malik, Niall Horan, Liam Payne, and Harry Styles. They formed on season seven of the British version of *The X Factor*, placed third, were snapped up by bigwig record boss Simon Cowell, released a bunch of hits, and less than six months after releasing their first single became the first band from the U.K. whose debut album grabbed the Number One spot in America.

The fresh-faced, floppy-haired five-piece have been compared to another one-time handsome pop group who sported mop-top hair and brought Europe, America, and the rest of the world to a standstill—The Beatles. In fact, 1D Delirium is threatening to out-squeal, out-chase, and out-faint Beatlemania in its heyday.

In a teeny-weeny space of time, the boys have gone from reality TV underdogs to signing a mega-bucks record contract and becoming international heartthrobs. Now, their faces are plastered all over bedroom walls and book covers around the world, their tours sell out in minutes, they've accumulated millions of Facebook and Twitter fans, racked up gazillions of YouTube hits, been turned into plastic dolls, acquired armfuls of shiny trophies—including a BRIT award (British equivalent of a Grammy)—and have tons of exciting plans in the pipeline.

The boys may still have some way to go before stealing The Beatles' pop crown, but they show no signs of giving up—and, in storming to the top of the U.S. album charts with their first album, they've achieved something even the legendary George, Paul, John, and Ringo couldn't. Directioners, the competition is on!

Left: One Direction at RTL 2 TV Music Show, The Dome, Duisburg, Germany, November 2011
Below: In concert at Heaven nightclub, London, September 2011

HARRY

Name: Harry Edward Styles
Born: February 1, 1994
Cheshire, England

Harry Styles' name couldn't be more fitting. It sums up the singer down to a tight, white tee: a super-cute Brit boy and, thanks to a wardrobe full of said t-shirts, bow ties, and trendy chinos—ultra cool.

The baby of 1D, Harry was born Harry Edward Styles on February 1, 1994. He was welcomed by parents Anne and Des and older sister Gemma, in Cheshire, England. It should come as no surprise to learn that the curly-haired crooner—perhaps the one who makes the most Directioners scream—was also an adorable little boy. "He was so pretty as a baby," mommy Styles cooed in a newspaper interview. Not only was Harry cute and a model student at school, he also loved music. He played the part of Buzz Lightyear in the school's production of *Chitty Chitty Bang Bang* and when he was 14, he entered a Battle of the Bands competition at his school—as lead singer of a group named White Eskimo, with his friends Haydn, Nick, and Will. The group won the competition and the thrill of playing music for people reinforced Harry's desire to be a full-time pop star.

When he was 16, Harry ventured to the 2010 *X Factor* auditions (in the U.K.). Life for the bright student, who was preparing to go to college, was about to drastically change. Harry never made it past Boot Camp as a solo artist, of course—but that turned out to be the making of 1D. It was clever Harry who came up with the band name, telling the others it would sound amazing being boomed out across the live TV studio audience by the powerful-lunged *X Factor* voice-over man—and the others all agreed.

Harry's looks, singing voice, and bubbly personality means he's a hit with the ladies. He's never short of female fans or gal pals. He's also single and ready—similar to the words of the band's biggest hit—to light up the world of somebody else. The best news? Harry says he'd have no problem dating a fan!

Harry gives direction at Radio City Music Hall, New York, March 2012 ★★★★

Liam might not be the oldest member of the group, but to the other guys he's like a big brother: he's the level-headed, focused one who gets them organized and acts sensible when needed.

It's not surprising that the chocolate-button-eyed 19-year-old has a mature head on his shoulders: he was forced to grow up quickly due to a childhood illness. He was born to mom Karen and dad Geoff on August 29, 1993, in Wolverhampton, England. After spending his early years in and out of the hospital and enduring numerous tests, doctors discovered the cause of his illness—only one of Liam's kidneys worked. But Liam never let his illness get him down. He just became more determined.

Liam loved to sing and enjoyed nothing better than crooning along to the radio and playing karaoke computer games—he loved Justin Timberlake and Take That's music in particular. At school, he also tried out for sports teams and all the other pursuits that boys love. But Li and soccer balls never became the best of friends:

instead, he discovered that he was a super cross-country runner, and at 12, he became a member of the school's under-18s team, winning races left and right. For a while, Liam dreamt of being an Olympic runner. He also got into boxing after becoming the target of a few bullies at school. But, despite being great in both a pair of sneakers and a pair of boxing gloves, Liam wasn't destined to be a star of the track or the ring. He had other dreams.

Liam was a regular in the school choir from an early age, and at 14, he decided to audition for England's version of *The X Factor*. He didn't make it past the Judges' Houses, and he was crushed. But thank goodness he didn't—because as we all know now, it was just a matter of time before Li returned to the show and found his true direction.

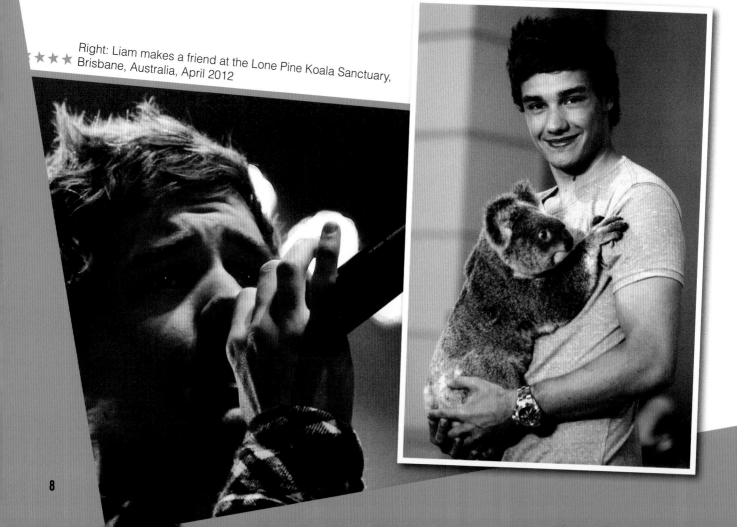

★★★ Right: Liam makes a friend at the Lone Pine Koala Sanctuary, Brisbane, Australia, April 2012

LIAM

LOUIS

Name: Louis William Tomlinson
Born: December 24, 1991
Doncaster, England

Louis was a great early Christmas present for his mom and dad. The oldest member of 1D was born on Christmas Eve 1991, to folks Johannah and Troy in Doncaster, England.

His mom and dad split up when Louis and his sister Charlotte were young and his mom later married Louis' stepdad Mark Tomlinson (whose surname Louis took). As a young boy, Louis yearned for brothers to play with, but it wasn't meant to be. Mark was dad to three young daughters, so Louis inherited a gang of sisters instead: Félicité—also known as "Fizzy"—and twins Daisy and Phoebe. Like a typical good big bro, Louis was supportive and protective of his sisters, and while he might not have gotten as much soccer practice with them as he might have with boys, growing up in a house of ladies had a positive effect on him. As a result, he says he understands girls better now and is more sensitive. In fact, Louis regularly gets teased by the rest of the boys for his big, mushy love of babies.

Louis is a funny, outgoing guy and could have been a comedic actor in another life—if a One Direction member is going to spring a practical joke, you can bet it'll be him. At school, he showed early signs of talent for the performing arts, landing singing parts in school productions and a few small TV roles. Performing was obviously in his DNA.

Louis was a good student, but his grades suffered in his later years because he partied too much. He landed himself a job as a waiter before *X Factor*, which he admits he wasn't exactly good at: he spilled bowls of soup and splashed drinks down diners' clothes, but he was popular with lady customers and admits he made good tips because he was good at flirting! This made him the perfect candidate for his next role: singer in a super-hot, chart-smashing boy band.

Now not only has Louis found his true calling, he finally got the gang of brothers he always wanted.

Louis makes some noise at Radio City Music Hall, New York, March 2012 ★★★★★

Imagine shaking a can of soda really hard and then opening it right away. That's Niall's personality for you. The only Irish guy in the band, this bubbly blue-eyed boy was born on September 13, 1993 to Maura and Bobby.

Niall has an older brother Gregg, whom he argued with lots until they both hit their teens—after which they had a much better relationship. Despite his mom and dad splitting when he was little, the two—along with Niall's stepdad Chris—get along really well now. And Niall credits 1D's success in bringing them together.

Niall was not very academic and never attended his school prom. He was more interested in entertaining and always looked like he had what it took to become a superstar singer. He was a constant fixture in the school choir and was always singing along to songs on the radio. When he received a guitar one Christmas as a young boy... that was it: his ambition to become a pop star was cemented. Growing up, he put together a varied MP3 playlist. Alongside the latest pop acts, sat classics from Frank Sinatra to Bon Jovi, but as Niall hit his

mid-teens he fell in love with Michael Bublé's music—and meeting him a couple of years later on *The X Factor* was like a dream come true. Niall is also a self-confessed Belieber and screamed when the Bieb' started following him on Twitter.

One of the chattiest members of 1D, Niall is never quiet when he's with the band, but he never talks much during interviews. He is worried that he'll say the wrong thing. When the band travels to the States, the loudest screams are always for the Irish boy. According to U.S. fans, Niall has the perfect combo of Irish charm and wholesome looks. Well... we could have told them that!

In concert at The Beacon Theatre, New York, May 2012 ★ ★ ★ ★ ★

A thoughtful Niall at a radio interview in Sydney, Australia, April 2012

NIALL

ZAYN

Name: Zayn Jawaad Malik
Born: January 12, 1993
Bradford, England

Bradford-born Zayn is often thought of as the "bad boy" of One Direction—and although he's got several tattoos, and comes across as quiet and mysterious sometimes, Zayn is a softie underneath and can be just as funny and mischievous as Louis and Niall when he sets his mind to it.

Zayn, whose name means "beautiful" in Arabic, was born on January 12, 1993 to British mom Tricia and British-Pakistani dad Yaser. He has three sisters: older sister Doniya and younger sisters Waliyha and Safaa. Like Louis, Zayn says growing up in a houseful of girls has made him more sensitive and comfortable around the opposite sex. Good news, Directioners!

During his school years, Zayn was popular, but preferred to hang out with a couple of very close friends rather than as part of a massive group. He was also studious and excelled in poetry, reading, and writing. His love of writing hasn't taken a back seat since joining 1D. In fact, he says it's helped him with his songwriting. He loves being in the studio more than anything, and finds that penning tunes is similar to writing poems at school.

Shy one minute, and confident the next, Zayn showed an early talent for singing and performing, and famously starred in a school production of *Grease* alongside his friend and future *West is West* lead actor Aqib Khan. Needless to say, the talented teen had his fair share of female admirers at school. And the love hasn't died down since he joined the band.

Zayn's music teachers spotted his potential early on, and urged him to apply for *The X Factor* when he was 15 and 16. Luckily for us, Zayn only felt ready to audition when he was 17. The rest, as they say, is history.

On NBC's Today Show, New York, March 2012

Zayn in his hometown of Bradford, England, December 2010

They may be world-conquering pop princes strutting their stuff on stage, but when you think about it, it wasn't so long ago that the 1D boys were just toddlers running around in diapers. Youngest of the bunch Harry Styles' first memories are of going to Disney Land and hanging out at his nursery school, Happy Days.

Harry's mom and dad split up when he was only seven, and he took it very hard. But, the happy-go-lucky boy wasn't sad for long: when he and his mom and sis moved out into the countryside to live above a pub (where his mom was the landlady), he made friends with an older boy named Reg and they spent their summers riding their bikes through the country trails and visiting their favorite ice cream shop—which Harry took the 1D boys to when they all stayed at his mom's house during *X Factor* Boot Camp.

And it's not surprising to learn that Harry was a hit with girls from an early age. In a newspaper interview, Harry's dad said, "We went on holiday once to Cyprus when he was nine and as we left there was a whole melee of teenage girls, 16, 17-year-olds gathered by the side of the bus saying, 'Bye Harry, we love you.' Clearly he's a bit special."

Clever Zayn—or should we say Brainy Zayny—could mostly be found with his head in a book when he was a young boy. When he was eight, experts told him he had the reading level of an 18-year-old, so his proud granddad used to encourage him to read aloud to the family.

One of Niall's earliest memories was when his mom and dad split up when he was five. He had to change schools, but the outgoing boy, who once owned a Teletubbies onesie (cringe), won his new pals over with his great sense of humor.

Louis was a jokester in elementary school. He says he wasn't exactly naughty but he loved playing the class clown. He was a Power Rangers fanatic, and when he moved to Poole, England, for a couple of years when he was young, he loved it because the local arcade had Power Rangers rides and games.

It might be hard to believe, but well-behaved Liam was a total rebel during his early years at school. The curly-haired hottie admits he got into lots of trouble while in school, and he was punished for climbing on the school roof and instigating numerous water fights.

You can't say that those One Direction boys don't surprise us!

Niall developed a great sense of humor very early in life ★ ★ ★ ★ ★

THE EARLY YEARS

Right: Louis visits his old school Hall Cross in Doncaster, England, in December 2010

Below: Harry with a childhood photo of himself in his hometown of Cheshire, England, December 2010 ★ ★ ★ ★ ★

HOME

Home is where the 1D boys' hearts are and whenever they get the chance, they go back to catch up with their old friends.

Louis heads back to Doncaster in South Yorkshire to see his old Hayfield School and Hall Cross School friends. Harry hops home to the pretty area of Holmes Chapel in Cheshire. Niall jets over to Edgeworthstown, County Longford in Ireland to see his mom, and to Mullingar to see his dad and his old school friends from the Christian Brothers School. Liam heads back to Wolverhampton to re-connect with his pals and big sisters Ruth and Nicola, while Zayn heads up north to East Bowling in Bradford to chill out with his family and old school pals from Tong High School.

The boys love their home comforts and get to recharge their super-strength batteries as soon as they shut the front door behind them. Of course, behind every great 1D boy is a great mom. Aside from bringing the five hotties into the world, the 1D moms provide the boys with love, support, and even cups of tea for the fans who camp outside their houses.

Harry's mom, Anne Cox—or Foxy Coxy—is the most famous 1D mom, and has over 200,000 followers on Twitter. Liam's mom, Karen, is so proud of her son she often ends up in tears—if she'd carried a bucket around with her during Li's *X Factor* auditions, she could have filled it and had enough to water her garden. Louis is super-close to his beloved mom, Johanna—AKA Jay. They text all the time and she calls him "Boo." Cute. Zayn's mom, Tricia, might have Zayn's sisters Doniya, Waliyha, and Safaa to look after, but that doesn't stop her from traveling down to his pad in London to do his chores. She also has a cell phone case with Zayn's picture on it! And finally, Niall's mom, Maura: her proudest moment came when Niall flew her to the U.S. to one of the band's gigs and she was confronted with American girls chanting Niall's name at the top of their lungs!

★★★★ One Direction visit Hall Cross School in Doncaster, England, where Louis was once a student.

The boys visit Harry's home in Holmes Chapel, Cheshire, in December 2010 ★★★★★★★★

THE X FACTOR: SOLO HOPEFULS

The 1D boys first went to *The X Factor* auditions in 2010 hoping to make it as solo stars.

In Manchester, England, 16-year-old Harry showed up with his mom—who wore a special "Harry has X Factor" t-shirt. Showing early star quality, Harry sang Stevie Wonder's "Isn't She Lovely" and the girls in the crowd swooned. Former Pussycat Doll Nicole Scherzinger, who was a guest judge, loved it. "For 16 years old, you have a beautiful voice," she told him. Simon Cowell was equally impressed. Judge Louis Walsh was the exception; he thought Harry was too young to go through to Boot Camp, but it didn't matter: Simon and Nicole put him through.

Liam's *X Factor* 2010 audition was a case of second-time luck. Unlike in 2008 when he auditioned wearing his older sister's boyfriend's oversized jeans and looking nervous, the 16-year-old looked cool and composed in a fashionable outfit. He sang "Cry Me A River"—not the Justin Timberlake version, but a jazzy blues song by an old singer named Ella Fitzgerald. Little did the judging panel know that the feeling he put into his performance had quite a lot to do with the fact that he recently found out a girl he liked had kissed another boy behind his back. The judges were unanimous: Li was through.

At 17, Zayn took the stage and sang Mario's "Let Me Love You" and, again, the panel were decided: Yes!

And, the same went for 18-year-old Louis who sang "Hey There, Delilah" by The Plain White Ts. Niall sang Ne-Yo's "So Sick" and Cheryl Cole gave his performance the thumbs-down. Thankfully, though, guest judge Katy Perry gave it a big thumbs-up: Niall was through, too.

The next stage of the competition was boot camp, but despite amazing performances from Harry and Liam of Oasis's "Stop Crying Your Heart Out," the panel decided not to send them through to the Judges' Houses stage. Zayn had a meltdown when it came to performing a group dance during his boot camp audition, and he hid backstage until Simon Cowell persuaded him to try again—but his moves clearly didn't impress the judges enough, because his name was not called out from the list of lucky contestants who made it to the next round. Niall and Louis' names weren't called either. All five boys had missed out, and all five were devastated. Until... the shock twist! Five boys and four girls were called back to face the panel of Simon, Nicole Scherzinger, and Louis Walsh. "You were too talented for us to let you go," said Nicole. They were all given another chance—but this time as members of a boy and girl band.

The boys prepare to join forces in 2010 ★★★★★

And so a band was born. Liam, Louis, Harry, Niall, and Zayn had a couple of weeks to get to know each other before the Judges' Houses stage of the competition. But because they were all from different parts of the country, it was going to be tricky.

Fortunately, the Styles family had a plan: the boys could all move into the bungalow that Harry's mom and stepdad Robin had in their yard. Their new pad might only have had one bedroom, but Harry's mom, Anne, filled it with blow-up mattresses so all the guys had somewhere to lay their weary heads. The bungalow also boasted its own swimming pool, and was the perfect place for the boys to hang out, and get to know each other.

Without a singing coach on hand, the boys admitted they were fairly clueless when it came to band rehearsals—they weren't sure which type of songs to rehearse (they sang a lot of Bruno Mars and Jason Derulo back then) and they were in the dark about how to harmonize. But those couple of weeks living together were invaluable in allowing them to bond—not to mention giving them a taste of what life would

be like if they got through to the live show stages of the competition and moved into the *X Factor* house.

At Simon Cowell's sun-baked house in Marbella, Spain, the boys sang Natalie Imbruglia's "Torn" for Simon and his sidekick Sinitta. Liam and Harry sang lead vocals, and while the boys looked a little nervous, they sounded great and were a natural fit as a group. "They're cool, they're relevant," Simon said as soon as they walked away. They were through! During the live auditions, the boys were a success week after week, performing hits by everyone from Bryan Adams to Rihanna, and putting their own unique 1D spin on them. The number of squealing fans swelled each week and the screams in the live audience got louder and louder. With just two weeks left of the competition to go, mentor Simon told them, "You are the most exciting band in the country." It all boded very well for the new band.

★★★★★ Right: The boys show off a variety of coordinating styles. Below: The band with Simon Cowell.

GETTING SIGNED / X FACTOR TOUR

The weeklong build-up to *The X Factor* 2010 two-night final was frenzied. Liam, Niall, Harry, Louis, and Zayn seemed to smile from every magazine and newspaper on the newsstand, and TV presenters were talking like the boys had already won the competition.

1D, Rebecca Ferguson, Matt Cardle, and Cher Lloyd all made the final, and the boys got to sing "She's The One" alongside Liam's idol Robbie Williams. It was a career highlight. When the audience votes were announced on Saturday night, you could cut the tension with a knife. First to go home was Cher. But, then came the shocker: the following night, *X Factor* host Dermot announced that 1D were eliminated. The boys were devastated, but determined. "This isn't the end of One Direction," assured Zayn as the *X Factor* TV audience cheered for them. It was just the beginning, agreed Simon.

As soon as they went backstage, the tears began to flow. Only Liam held it together because he'd been in the same situation before, and he had an inkling there was more to come. Soon after the live show ended, the 1D boys were called to Simon's office. They were as anxious to hear what he had to say as they had been at the Judges' Houses. Full of nerves, the boy-tears were ready to spring again. But, they shouldn't have been so worried. Simon told them he wanted to sign them in a megabucks

deal. He believed they could be huge. The boys jumped and cheered with excitement.

The following January, the boys were whisked off to Los Angeles, California, for five days to record tracks for their debut album. It was the first time any of them had been to the sun-drenched streets of LA, and they had an amazing time. Despite being away for less than a week, and having never released a single, the boys were greeted with crazy scenes when they touched down at Heathrow Airport, with hundreds of girls grabbing at them and their clothes. It got so insane that their tour manager, Paul, had to drive them out of the airport in a police riot van. They would need to get used to it. By the time the *X Factor* tour kicked off in Birmingham, Engand, in Spring 2011, hordes of poster-wielding fans turned out for 1D, and their eardrum-breaking squeals and chants rocketed off the Richter scale.

Left: *X Factor* Live at the LG Arena, Birmingham, England, February 2011

X Factor tour wrapped, the next mission for the boys was finishing the album and releasing a debut single.

"What Makes You Beautiful" was released in September 2011 and—O.M.G—zoomed straight to No 1. It was the fastest-selling single of the year, moving 150,000 copies in its first seven days. The boys easily beat the previous record holder, Bruno Mars—whose single "Grenade" sold 149,000 copies. Which is funny, considering it was one of the songs they used to practice singing when they first formed the band.

"What Makes You Beautiful" is a love song to a girl who doesn't realize how beautiful she is. And because she doesn't know it, and is actually quite shy, she becomes even more beautiful in the eyes of the boys—especially when she flips her hair! The track was accompanied by a video filmed on the beach. We see the boys messing around and having fun on Malibu Beach in California (jealous?)

and also in one-on-one close-ups with individual girls. We imagine that a few Harry fans' hearts fluttered during the part of the video where he stares deeply into one girl's eyes while singing to her.

The boys set up a challenge for themselves: to create music that didn't sound like a traditional boy band's—something unique. And they passed. While the single was a catchy, up-tempo pop record, it also managed to throw some cool guitars in there too, while giving tribute to the sounds of classic bands, such as The Beatles.

The song wasn't just massive in England, it also topped the Irish and Scottish charts, and went Top 10 in Belgium, Canada, and even Down Under in New Zealand and Australia. The wheels on world domination were already in motion!

★ ★ ★ One Direction greet fans at Oxford Circus, London, September 2011

On a video shoot in Anglesey, Wales in January 2012

A cake presented to the boys at Heaven nightclub, London September 2011 ★ ★ ★ ★ ★

CONGRATULATIONS! UKs Number One

U.K. TOUR

The screams almost lifted the roof off the Wolverhampton Civic Hall—and that was before the boys even appeared on stage.

It was the first official night of the Up All Night Tour, on December 21, 2011, and the Directioners were definitely up for it. It was a momentous occasion. As soon as the band appeared on stage, the crowd erupted into even more deafening screams while the venue exploded with the bright lights of hundreds of camera phones.

Many fans camped outside the venue, battling the winter weather since the early hours of that morning, but they showed no signs of tiredness. For a few seconds, 1D—backed by a live band—looked shell-shocked. "Wow!" they beamed in unison.

And then it was down to business. The boys kicked off with "Na Na Na" and the stage was transformed into a beach scene, complete with a VW camper. Later on in the set, the boys sat around a campfire to sing acoustic versions of some of their biggest hits. They also threw in some surprises, belting out covers of The Zutons' "Valerie," Natalie Imbruglia's "Torn," and Black Eyed Peas' "I Gotta Feelin."

The second part of the show featured the boys going back to school and becoming immersed in a winter wonderland—at one point fake snow flakes began to fall from the ceiling, which of course resulted in a big, fake snowball fight with the fans! They saved "What Makes You Beautiful" for last, before performing an encore where gold streamers floated from the roof and covered the crowd.

When tickets for the tour went on sale the previous September, they sold out in minutes! And the excitement of the fans was clear to see—and hear—on every subsequent date of the tour, which wrapped up in Belfast, Ireland, on January 26. Next stop: the world!

★★ The boys gather at St. Pancras Station, London in February 2012

U.K. FANS

As we all know, 1D's U.K. fans are legends—they've followed the boys through every step of their journey—from jittery *X Factor* hopefuls, to the globe-straddling pop phenomenon they are now.

The U.K. fans were there way before the boys even released a single, watching videos on YouTube, sharing news and gossip on Facebook, sending gifts, and following the boys on Twitter.

The U.K. fans came up with their own name too: the Directioners. By 2012, the boys' loyal band of followers had helped Liam, Louis, Zayne, and Niall rack up over four million fans each on Twitter, and helped propel Monsieur Styles to the five million mark. The U.K. Directioners also make up a huge chunk of the boys' nearly eight million Facebook fans and have helped the boys rack up BILLIONS of YouTube views! The U.K. fans have been there since the early days of *The X Factor*. They used to show up at the studios in north London to chant their support for the boys before the shows, and to try to catch a glimpse of them before they took to the stage.

As for the band, their message to the fans is: "Gotta be you!" The boys constantly give shout-outs to the Directioners, saying they'd be nowhere without them. In fact, it seems the boys take almost as much interest in the fans as the Directioners do in them. "We have different types of fans," says Zayn. "You have the ones that'll come up and scream... Then you'll have the ones that are more chilled out and want to have a conversation with you... And then you get the ones that are nervous and stare at you before screaming and running off."

Whichever category you fall into, the good news is that the boys are all open to romance with the right girl. Zayn says, "I don't think you should ever date someone depending on whether they're a fan or not. If they're a fan, it's cool. It wouldn't stop us." Form a line, ladies!

★ ★ ★ ★ ★ A selection of loyal fans from Doncaster and Manchester, England, showing their devotion

Top from left to right: Taylor Swift, Katy Perry, Nicole Scherzinger

Bottom: Harry sends a subtle message out to Kim Kardashian during a radio interview in Pennsylvania

★ ★ ★

GIRLS

Question: Do girls love 1D more than 1D love girls? It's an impossible one to answer! Not exactly short in the "looks" department, One Direction's whole life is sound-tracked by the swoons and screams of devoted female fans.

But the boys do their fair share of swooning back (just not the screaming part.) In no particular order, the boys have confessed to group crushes on Katy Perry, Cheryl Cole, and Nicole Scherzinger.

Single Harry is the most vocal when it comes to who he likes, and it's no secret that he likes older women—as proved by his three-month, highly controversial relationship with an older television personality named Caroline Flack. Harry has also confessed to having crushes on Kim Kardashian, Angelina Jolie, Kate Moss, and Kate Winslett. He's also been linked to Taylor Swift and Rita Ora—both of whom crush on him back.

Like Harry, Zayn dated an older woman after *The X Factor*—his show rival and 2010 runner-up, Rebecca Ferguson. And in 2011, news broke that he was dating Perrie Edwards from *X Factor* 2011's winning band, Little Mix. He certainly loves the *X Factor* ladies! In the early days, Perrie and Zayn Tweeted about their dates for the world to see—and they even kissed in public!

Niall, the shyest member of the band when it comes to girls, has been linked to none other than Hollywood hottie Demi Lovato. "We've spoken. She's a cool girl so I got in contact with her," he said sheepishly.

But while Liam and Louis went to see Katy Perry's movie—Tweeting all the way through about how great

of a singer she is—they both love nothing more than being settled down with a long-term GF. Louis' lady, Eleanor Calder, is such a big part of his life that she's often referred to as the sixth member of 1D—and they're always photographed having tearful goodbyes or happy hellos in airports. Liam, meanwhile, living up to his reputation as the most mature boy in the band, has moved into a pad with his girlfriend, Danielle Peazer.

But no matter who the boys date, kiss, move in with, or crush on, Directioners will always remain Directioners, and their fan base—massive!

Caroline Flack ★★★★★

BROMANCE

Directioners love a 1D bromance almost as much as they love the thought of going out with one of the boys themselves.

Bromance of course means a close but non-romantic friendship between two guys—and the most famous non-romantic love affair going on in 1D is between Harry and Louis. The two are so close that the fans have mashed their names together to form one: "Larry Stylinson." The boys fell into their bromance almost as soon as they met on *The X Factor*.

In his own words, Harry says, "Since we started at the *X Factor* House, me and Louis always said we wanted to move in together. And that was it, it pretty much just happened." He even joked in one interview that Louis was his celebrity crush. The bromance continued when the boys moved into a bachelor pad—one with its own movie room no less. And like any good couple, they look after each other. "Harry has rung me and said, 'Tea is ready!' so I don't cook a lot. I suppose I should start, but Harry's so good I don't need to," Louis said.

The two are so close that some fans initially thought "Larry" were in an actual relationship, which makes them LOL. A lot. They might not be actual boyfriends, but Harry's mom, Anne says their friendship is the real deal. "They're like brothers, they genuinely respect and love each other... At Christmas they had three days off from the band but Louis was on the phone to H to see what he was doing. They definitely have a bromance." Too cute.

The other members of the band are all prone to a bromance, too. Being such great friends, they're always hugging, laughing, and going to the movies with each other. The fans have come up with names for all the possible bromances within the band. Say hello to Zarry, Narry, Lirry, Lilo, Nouis, Zouis, Ziall, Ziam, and Niam!

★ ★ ★ ★ ★ Louis pretends to punch Niall during a concert in Mexico City, June 2012

Right: Fans call best buds, Louis and Harry, "Larry Stylinson".

Below: At the studios of BBC Radio 1, August 2011 ★★★

AMERICA: THE BEGINNING PART 1

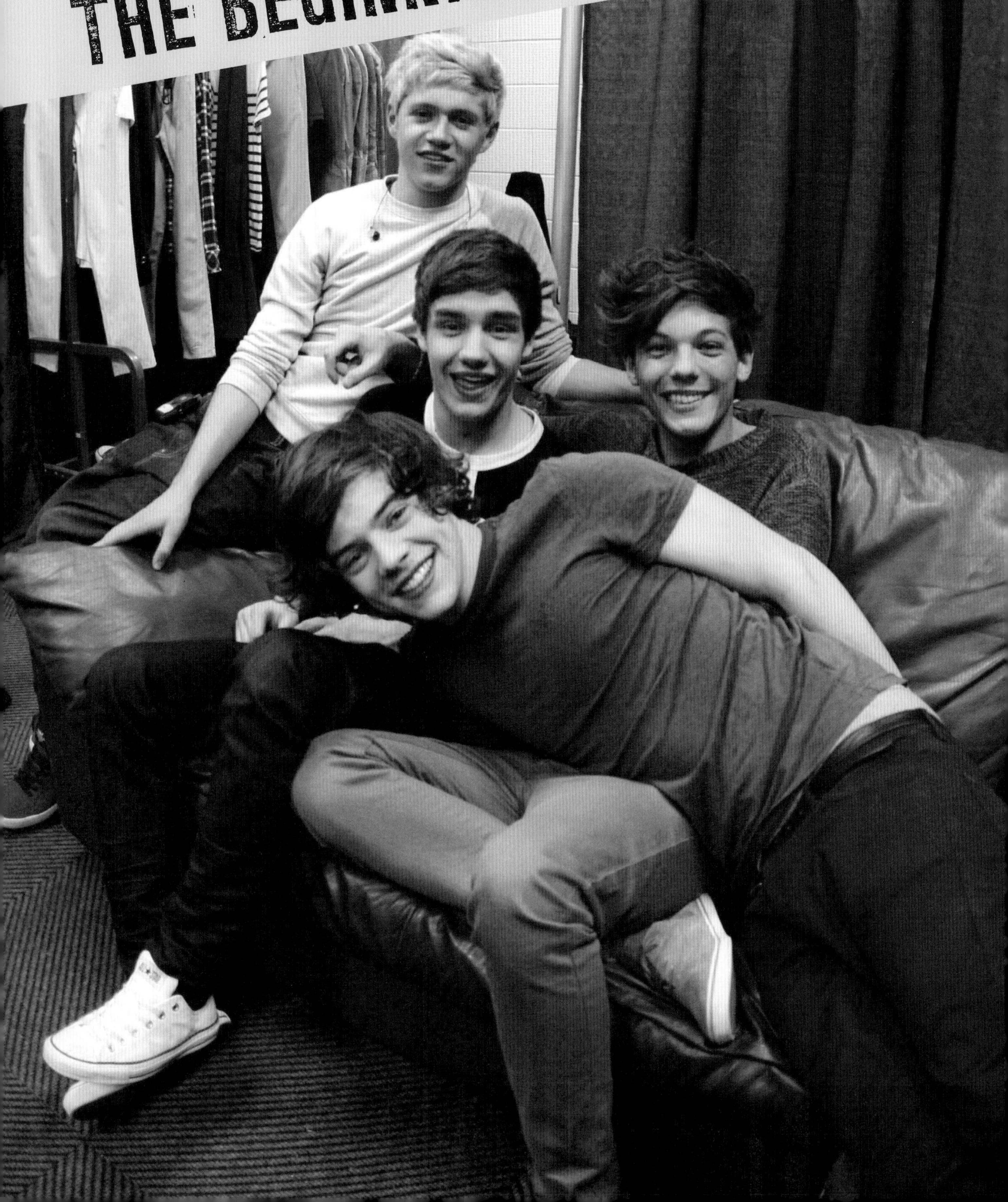

The crazy reaction to 1D in England told both the boys and their management that they were ready to take on America—and this was just a couple of months into their life as a bona fide band.

In November 2011, the band signed a deal with top U.S. record label Columbia, and in January, they got a call from the producers of the *Today* show who wanted them to appear on the show in March. The boys almost had to pinch themselves to make sure this wasn't a dream.

And that wasn't all—the boys then got a call from U.S. boy band Big Time Rush asking them to support them on their U.S. tour in February. BTR have their own Nickelodeon show and had already scored some big chart hits, so 1D knew the call was a big one. And then came another phone call, this time from the producers of the popular sitcom *iCarly* who wanted the boys to film a guest appearance in January. 1D Delirium was building in America, and their U.S. Facebook page was attracting thousands of new fans by the day. When the boys touched down at LAX, LA airport, to film their *iCarly*

scenes, they were greeted by 500 squealing fans. Another 200 or so screaming ladies then managed to squeeze their way onto the *iCarly* set to chant even more.

By the time the boys landed in Toronto, Canada, in February, for the Big Time Rush tour, One Direction mania had truly taken hold. When they appeared on Canadian show *MuchMusic,* they brought the city to a standstill, and its main road had to be closed off due to thousands of excited fans clogging it up.

Things got even more insane when they hit the road with BTR. They played 14 dates, wrapping up in Orlando, Florida, at the end of February and the momentum surrounding the band simmered, sizzled, and then exploded! Not only did fans flock out of venues with beaming smiles on their faces, but the critics loved 1D, too.

Left: Backstage at the Patriot Center in Virginia, March 2012
Below: Onstage at the Patriot Center

Once the tour was over, 1D had their album promo duties to carry out. In Boston at the Natrick Mall, a brain-boggling 5,000 fans turned up. The boys were absolutely shocked.

After that, they had their *Today* appearance to look forward to. Originally, the boys were scheduled for a normal in-studio performance at the famous 30 Rock TV studio in Rockerfeller Center in New York City. However, once news leaked to U.S. Directioners, producers were forced to relocate the appearance to the outdoor Rockefeller Plaza—the ice-skating rink area that has appeared in tons of romantic, Big Apple-based flicks.

The fans' excitement had reached a boiling point—social networking sites were abuzz, and U.S. Directioners planned to come out in full force. And that was when the New York Police Department got involved. When 1D arrived in midtown Manhattan on March 12—a day before the release of their album in the States—a gigantic 10,000-plus crowd descended on the plaza and spilled out onto the surrounding streets. The show's team was flabbergasted; they'd only ever seen scenes as crazy as this for Justin Bieber and Lady GaGa—the difference was, both of those artists had been long-established when they played, with a string of hits under their belts. After the show, fans chased the band's tour bus through the busy yellow-cab-crammed streets, threatening to overturn it with wild abandon when it stopped at traffic lights. Fortunately, they didn't, and the boys got to have a laugh at the craziness of it all.

Today producer Melissa Lonner gasped, "One Direction is relatively unknown with no hits yet. They basically exploded, and all the adults are saying, 'Who are these people, and how do they know about it?'"

They were about to find out a lot more!

★ ★ ★ ★ ★ Below: *The Today Show*'s Toyota Concert Series, New York, March 2012
Right: Liam and Zayn at an album signing in New York, March 2012

AMERICA: THE BEGINNING
PART 2

AMERICA: BREAKING RECORDS, MAKING HISTORY

In March 2012, 1D made U.S. chart history when they became the first U.K. group to debut at the top of the *Billboard* album charts.

Not even the likes of Coldplay, the Spice Girls—or a little-known band called The Beatles—managed this. In its first week, *Up All Night* sold almost 180,000 copies, while "What Makes You Beautiful" was climbing up the singles chart with gusto. The highest new entry for an album from a U.K. act before *Up All Night* was *Spice* by the Spice Girls, which landed at No. 6 in February 1997, before it traveled to the top. It was official: America loved 1D!

Tickets for the U.S. leg of the Up All Night Tour sold like half-price McDonald's burgers in a sea of hungry teens—they'd been snapped up almost as soon as they went on sale. 1D Delirium was as big, if not bigger, than Bieber Fever, and the boys' mind-blowing, sudden fame was now being compared to The Beatles'.

The media compared the band's arrival in the States to the crazy scenes when the legendary four-piece arrived in the U.S. for the first time in 1964.

But, while the boys were blown away by the attention and support, the down-to-earth posse didn't let The Beatles comparisons go to their heads. In a newspaper interview, Harry said, "That seems ridiculous to us, because they were such icons. But we watched a film of their first U.S. trip and there were similarities. We're as close as them despite not being together long."

But, the boys do have a little while to go yet before they usurp the Beatles' throne. Come on, Directioners... let's keep up the support!

U.S. Fans at the Nickelodeon Annual Kids Choice Awards, Los Angeles, March 2012 ★★★★★

THE UP ALL NIGHT TOUR U.S.

By the time 1D arrived in Connecticut in May 2012 for the opening night of the U.S. leg of The Up All Night Tour, they were the name on everyone's lips.

Not only did 1D manage to snag a No. 1 spot on the album charts, and watch "What Makes You Beautiful" hit No. 4 in the singles charts, they also appeared on *Saturday Night Live* (which has millions and millions of viewers, so it wasn't bad for upping the boys' profile). On the show, they acted out a mock feud with rival Brit boy band The Wanted, whose single "Glad You Came" hit the No. 3 spot.

The U.S. fans loved the guys' show: the beachy first segment, the high school scenes, and the snowy final act where snowflakes fell from the sky (ceiling). A couple of nights into the tour, at the Patriot Center in Virginia, the sound of the girls' shrieks were recorded—and they clocked in at 122 decibels! That, you could say, is pretty loud. And while the boys bounced around on stage, the audience—in an array of t-shirts bearing messages from

"I love you, Niall" to "Mrs. Harry Styles"—threw glow sticks, baseball caps, teddy bears, and flags in their idols' direction.

As the tour continued, the hysteria increased—and fans found even more clever ways to get close to the boys. Including one fan who hid in the boys' garbage can at one of the venues where they were performing. Yup, you read that right. She hid in the trash in the hopes of sneaking through the back doors to see them. Imagine if she'd succeeded. Ew! Now, the boys' security team make sure to regularly check the garbage.

One group of American fans booked a room in the same hotel as the boys, while another went one step further, and dressed up as hotel staff in the hopes of catching a glimpse of Zayn, Niall, Harry, Liam, and Louis. Yikes!

★ ★ ★ ★ ★ Below: One Direction in concert at the Susquehanna Bank Center in New Jersey, May 2012
Right: Zayn and the boys perform at the Beacon Theater in New York in May 2012

Left: Showing their colors at Fountain Studios, London, November 2011

Below: A suited 1D at the *GQ* Men of the Year Awards, London, September 2011 ★ ★ ★

STYLE

The 1D boys have style and fashion sense by the bucket load. They also have five very distinct "looks" that reflect each of their personalities.

Having been in a band before One Direction, it's no surprise that Harry nailed the swaggering pop-star look from the get-go. Even when he showed up at the *X Factor* auditions back in 2010, he looked cool in his long, skinny scarf and big, curly rock-boy mop top. Now, Harry favors skinny jeans, tight t's, his trademark blazer with an embroidered "H," and when the mood strikes him, a bow tie.

Louis' fashion sense also stood out at the *X Factor* auditions—however, he's now swapped his famous bowl haircut for a super-cool messy short 'do. Back in 2010, Louis loved sporting a beanie hat and a denim shirt opened to reveal a t-shirt. Now he's known for rocking the nautical look, often wearing striped shirts and bright, skinny jeans or chinos. He has also been known to rock a pair of suspenders over his tight tees—which shouldn't work, but somehow does—probably because it reflects his killer sense of humor.

Style-conscious Zayn, with his super-slick coif, often looks like the lead from a Hollywood flick, so its no surprise that he favors an American "look." The sneaker fanatic has hundreds of pairs of high-tops, which he likes to wear with a pair of jeans and a varsity jacket bearing his name.

Down-to-earth Niall is more interested in having a laugh than looking like a *GQ* model or showing off his pecs, so he can usually be found in a buttoned-to-the-top polo shirt and pair of jeans. As for Liam? The boy loves to wear plaid shirts and jeans—and to leave his naturally curly hair big and messy.

The only time the boys ever threw us for a fashion loop was the time they wore matching onesies to catch a flight. Oh, and the time they swapped outfits to play a gig in New Zealand during the The Up All Night Tour. Niall in Louis' striped tee? Cute, but kinda confusing!

Zayn and Harry have some impressive tattoos ★ ★ ★ ★ ★

It took 1D less than six months to crack the U.S.—an accomplishment that has escaped the clutches of loads of popular U.K. artists.

For instance, Robbie Williams, who mentored the boys on the *X Factor* final, must have been green with envy watching them take the country by storm. Things went from amazing to even more amzaing in the States. In the summer of 2012, "What Makes You Beautiful" hit the 2 million sales mark in the U.S. Meanwhile, the boys' *Up All Night: The Live Tour DVD* became another record breaker when it was released in America—it was named the first music DVD to outsell the No. 1 Billboard album of the same week. While U.S. singer John Mayer's chart-topping album sold 65,000, 1D's DVD sold 76,000 copies. Yowzers!

But it wasn't just U.K. and U.S. fans who adored the boys. The five-piece were shooting cupid's arrows through the hearts of fans all around the globe. We all know how well *Up All Night* did in England and the States, but did you know it also topped the charts in these countries: Canada, Croatia, Ireland, Italy, Mexico, Sweden, New Zealand, and Australia? It hit the Top 10 in Belgium, Denmark, the Netherlands, Finland, Greece, Hungary, Poland, Portugal, Scotland, and Spain, and blasted into the Top 20 in Austria, the Czech Republic, France, Germany, Norway, and Switzerland.

Aussie fans are as crazy for the boys as the U.K. and U.S. Directioners. When the boys landed in Sydney in April to play a daytime TV show, the scenes were insane. The Sydney streets were filled with teenagers waving posters, and loudly declaring their love for the boys. It was the same outside the Four Seasons Hotel in Mexico, when the boys arrived in the country for the first time, and the same thing in Norway, when the boys were besieged by girls waving the national flag.

So, really it came as no surprise at all, when in June 2012, 1D's team announced that *Up All Night* had sold nearly three million copies around the world. Now, where else is there left to conquer, boys? Mars?

 Emotional fans in Sydney, Australia, April 2012

46

WORLD DOMINATION

Below: Jumping for joy. Fans at Hisense Arena, Melbourne, Australia, April 2012
Bottom: Causing a storm at the NRJ radio show, Paris, February 2012

SUCCESS AND AWARDS

It was February 21, 2012. The venue: London's O2 Arena. The occasion: the BRIT Awards, AKA the biggest night on the U.K. music awards calendar.

And Zayn Malik, Niall Horan, Louis Tomlinson, Liam Payne, and Harry Styles were sitting on one of the circular tables in the star-studded arena. One Direction had only released their first single six months prior to the show, but there they were, sitting with global pop megastars such as Adele and Rihanna.

The boys were up for Best British Single for "What Makes You Beautiful" alongside Adele's monster hit "Someone Like You" and The Wanted's "Glad You Came," among others. The humble boys crossed their fingers and toes, but didn't think they stood a chance of taking home the trophy. When Tinie Tempah came on stage to announce the winner, they were in for a surprise, however. Tinie called out their name and, as one, the boys leapt from their chairs. By the time they walked to the stage, they composed themselves, and looked every inch the classy chart-conquering group that they were. In coordinating suits, they thanked their fans and team.

Backstage at the BRITS press conference after the show, Harry gasped, "This part of our success is not normal. We're 18, 19, and 20. People like us don't get to do things like this very often. We're just so grateful for this massive opportunity." But there was one question the assembled media wanted to hear: which 1D boy was going to get to keep the trophy? "We're going to break it into five pieces," joked Louis. "I want its head," laughed Niall.

We wouldn't have blamed the boys for wanting to hit the town after their win, but the down-to-earth group celebrated by hitting up... McDonalds. "That's how normal we are," said Niall.

The BRIT was not the only award the boys received in 2012. They also took home Favorite U.K. Newcomer and Favorite U.K. Band at the Nickelodeon Kids' Choice Awards; and Best Group, Best Breakthrough, and Best Video for "What Makes You Beautiful" at the 4Music Awards. They were also recognized at the Teen Choice Awards and the MuchMusic Video Awards in America and Canada.

If they carry on like this, the boys are going to have to buy a new house just for all their awards.

Looking hot in the California sunshine at Nickelodeon's 25th Annual Kids Choice Awards, Los Angeles, March 2012

Above Left: One Direction at the BRITS award show, London, February 2012
Below Left: Performing at the BBC Radio 1 Teen Awards, London, October 2011

1D MERCHANDISE!

I ♥ 1D

ONE DIRECTION VIVID ONE DIRECTION VIVID ONE DIRE
DIRECTION VIVID ONE DIRECTION VIVID ONE DIRECTION
DIRECTION VIVID ONE DIRECTION VIVID ONE DIR
DIRECTION VIVID ONE DIRECTION VIVID ONE DI
RECTION ONE DIRECTION

ONE DIRECTIO

One Direction dolls greet the fans at the annual Toy Fair in Olympia, London, January 2012

It's not just records that 1D sell by the boat load. It seems their handsome faces can sell just about anything!

Back in 2011, Directioners were beyond excited when toy makers Hasbro announced that they were making plastic doll versions of the band. The boys' little look-a-likes became one of the most asked-for presents on Christmas lists that year. Santa fielded quite a few requests at his office in the North Pole, too. Along with books like this one, 1D's faces have also adorned pencil cases, cell phone cases, bracelets, necklaces, charms, earrings, mugs, plates, duvet covers, pencils, calendars, birthday cards, lunch boxes, and even edible cake toppers—so if you bought two, you really could have your 1D cake topper and eat it, too!

When the lads released their official 2012 calendar in December 2011, it became the top-selling calendar of all time, beating Cheryl Cole's Official Cheryl Cole 2011 Calendar and (whisper it…) the original *X Factor* boy band JLS's Official JLS 2011 Calendar. Well, having the boys' smiling faces beam out at you on a rainy weekend in March certainly lifts the spirits.

Whatever 1D touched, it turned to sparkly gold. In April 2011, the boys were asked to become brand ambassadors for Pokémon Black and White on the Nintendo DS, which wasn't too hard seeing as they already loved playing the game, and they also launched two limited edition Nokia phones containing exclusive 1D content.

Not only were they immortalized as dolls and cake decorations, the boys were also turned into cartoon characters. *The Adventurous Adventures of One Direction* is a piece of fan fiction created by a famous U.S. animator, and is a massive YouTube hit. In the cartoon, the five boys play superhero characters with an overlord based on the character of Simon Cowell. It wasn't just the fans who hearted it, the boys thought it was awesome, too. "We loved it," said Liam. "And there might be some more cartoons with our voices in the future." Is there anything the band can't do?

LIFE IN THE SPOTLIGHT

Since their chart debut, life for 1D has been an exhilarating whirl of touring, recording, rehearsing, promoting, jet-setting, and sightseeing—all accompanied by the pop of paparazzi flashbulbs and the eardrum-busting screams of their adoring fans—a dream come true for the five boys.

But while the boys regularly have to pinch themselves while experiencing how much life has changed for the better since hitting the big time, they admit that life in the spotlight can be tough, too. Niall, for instance, has revealed that being in the thick of 1D Delirium makes him nervous. The boys are besieged by girls clamoring and sometimes grabbing them wherever they go—and Niall once found himself in the middle of a fan frenzy as they tried to tear off his clothes. He admits, "I get really claustrophobic and sometimes it's a bit scary."

And while the boys love nothing more than flying around the world, visiting new countries, there is one downside: jet lag. Powering between different countries' time zones messes with their internal clocks, as Niall discovered after flying home after the band's tour Down

Under in Spring 2012. "Goodnight world! Love you all! The jab I got off jetlag today was digusting! Feel like I've done 12 rounds with tyson! #brickwall," he Tweeted.

Life is exciting for 1D, but not always glamorous. During particularly busy touring periods, the boys have been known to max two hours' sleep a night. And when the band finished the first leg of their Up All Night Tour in April 2012, they were shattered. "We're tired and need time to chill out," Harry snoozily told Radio 1.

But while the jetlag, fan mania, and all-nighters have left the boys feeling weary from time to time, they all know it's just a small price to pay for living their dream. As Zayn says, "Since we got put together, we've made four best friends… we're on the road and we do something that we love every single day, so for us that's the most amazing part."

★ ★ ★ Below: Making magic at the World Film Premiere of *Harry Potter and the Deathly Hallows: Part 1*, London, November 2011
Right: Besieged by fans at Real Radio, Manchester, U.K. in August 2011

DOWNTIME

1D might love their day job, but they love just hanging out, too. And when the boys aren't touring or doing TV or radio, they certainly know how to make the most of their spare time.

Harry loves nothing more than taking a flashy sportscar for a spin. During the boys' tour of the States in summer 2012, the curly-haired hottie was photographed whizzing around the streets in a black Ferrari worth a whopping $190,000. No surprise he's treated himself to a fancy Audi R8! He's also learned to ski since joining the band.

When the boys toured Australia, they got a taste for yachts: sunbathing on them and diving from them! While on tour in the States, the boys took to the water again—this time to go fishing. Liam—despite picking up a fishing rod for only the second time in his life—caught a 20-foot shark (which he threw back into the water)! The brown-eyed boy couldn't contain his excitement. "We had such great fun," he bubbled. "We went fishing for half an hour and there was nothing at all. Then I pulled out a baby tiger shark."

When not on stage, Liam and Louis love taking part in activities that give them a different kind of adrenalin rush. And we're not just talking white-knuckle amusement park rides here—although they do love a theme park—we're talking dizzying 192-feet bungee jumps! They both did a jump when they visited Auckland in New Zealand in Spring 2012. Gulp.

It's not all superhero pastimes, though. The boys all have secret guilty pleasures, too. Harry loves unwinding watching Jeremy Kyle; Liam and Louis are obsessed with playing PlayStation; Zayn loves reading comic books and sketching; and Niall can often be found watching DVDs of his favorite Irish band Westlife. See, they're just like the rest of us after all!

The boys get some down time "down under" in April 2012

CELEB FANS

It's not just the hordes of adoring Directioners who love the boys, the band has a huge celeb fan base, too. One of their biggest fans—in every sense of the word but height—is pop phenomenon, Justin Bieber.

One minute Niall was rehearsing his songs during *X Factor* Boot Camp, and the next minute, the Biebs is following the guys on Twitter and telling anyone who'll listen how great they are.

"They look great, they sound great and, when you add their British accents into the mix, the American girls are going crazy for them," Biebs told one newspaper. "One Direction are genuine good guys. The industry needs a fresh boyband, and by the end of this year they will be the biggest boyband in the world." Biebs, who's good pals with pop princesses Carly Rae Jepson and Taylor Swift, also fessed, "I already know one of the biggest artists in the world thinks Harry is so hot, but I have been sworn to secrecy."

So it's not just infatuated Harry fans drawing hearts around his face… Rihanna's also in on the mix. "Harry, yeah. I watch their videos and I remember thinking, 'Wow, he's a star,'" she swooned in one interview. "He seems very sure. It seems, like, it's so natural to him."

Weirdly, badboy rapper Dappy can't get enough of the boys next door either. "As singers, they're just amazing. I love One Direction most definitely," he told Hits radio. Former Pussycat Doll Nicole Scherzinger, who was part of the *X Factor* judging panel that put the band together, says, "I keep patting myself on the back for it. They're five great singers and look great in a band."

And as if that weren't enough, The Beatles legend Paul McCartney is a fan and called them "the next terrific band." It doesn't end there! The boys have actually won over the First Lady of the United States. Michelle Obama and daughters Sasha and Malia are such huge fans of the boys that they reportedly invited them over to the White House for an Easter egg hunt!

First Lady Michelle Obama with daughters Sasha and Malia ★★★★★

★★★★★ Clockwise from left: Sir Paul McCartney, Rihanna, Justin Bieber, and Dappy

THE FUTURE

Throw on your sunglasses, Directioners: the boys' future is super bright. More chart-stopping albums, more awards, massive world tours, movies... The band is living in fast-forward and the world is their oyster.

With one globe-conquering album under their belts, the boys spent much of 2012 working on the pulse-quickening follow-up (which everyone from Brit boy Ed Sheeran to Justin Bieber wanted to play a part in), and with a grungier, grown-up feel, it became the boys' mission statement for 2013 and beyond. Their dream is to keep on writing their own tunes and one day, they would love to play their own instruments, too. Harry says, "We're always writing on the road and in hotels and airports. We don't ever want our music to sound like a 40-year-old man in an office has written it and given it to us to perform." No chance, boys.

The boys can't wait to take album number two's tunes on the road on their super-duper 2013 world tour either. Proving their fan base was growing ever-more ginormous, the tour sold out in seconds. And with over 100 shows around the world—including a six-night stint at London's O2 Arena—it was as big a deal for the Directioners as it was for the band. When the tour went on sale in the U.K. and Ireland in 2012, over 300,000 tickets were sold in the first day. The boys were forced to add additional dates to the North America leg too, due to hordes of U.S. Directioners stampeding for tickets. And when the tour went on sale in Australia and New Zealand, the ticket sales racked up millions of dollars, with all 190,000 tickets for all the dates selling out super-quick.

The boys are constantly working on exciting new ways to surprise us. There's even talk of them recruiting a sixth member—well, a four-legged one at least! The boys say they'd love nothing more than to take a 1D dog on tour with them. And with rumors constantly swirling about a future in the movies, there's loads of stuff for 1D devotees to be excited about. The boys are here to stay, Directioners. Hold on to the feeling, and don't let go…

★★★★★ The future looks very bright…

DID YOU KNOW...?

The boys call Liam "the Gary Barlow of the band."

Harry can juggle.

Harry wanted to be a lawyer.

Niall wanted to be a sound engineer.

The boys' 2013 world tour sold half a million tickets in two hours.

Liam can beatbox.

The first song Liam sang in public was "Let Me Entertain You" during a karaoke competition when he was six.

Zayn once played Bugsy in a school production of *Bugsy Malone*.

The Boys once dared Liam to sneak the words "Rodney" and "Del Boy" into one of their songs during *The X Factor* Tour—and he did.

Niall can speak French.

Louis is the messiest member of the band.

Louis was in a band at school named The Rogue.

Zayn had his first kiss standing on a brick.

Louis was suspended from school once and had to retake his senior year.

When the boys stayed in Harry's bungalow before *X Factor* Bootcamp, they lived on KFC.

Harry had his first girlfriend at the age of six—he bought her a teddy bear.

The boys' hit "What Makes You Beautiful" was featured in an episode of *Glee*.

Harry's hair was blonde when he was in preschool.

Niall is the band's biggest Tweeter.

If he didn't become a pop star, Liam wanted to be a firefighter.

Harry owns gold, snake-print underwear.

Niall once supported former *X Factor* contestant Lloyd Daniels on tour.

Liam is scared of spoons.

One of the band's career highlights is appearing on the Alan Titchmarsh show.

Zayn has nine tattoos and wants a "sleeve."

Louis sees himself having up to 20 kids if that's how many times it takes till he gets a boy.

When Liam was 12, he beat a professional adult runner in a cross-country race.

One of Liam's favorite toys as a little kid was his Buzz Lightyear doll.

1D Quiz

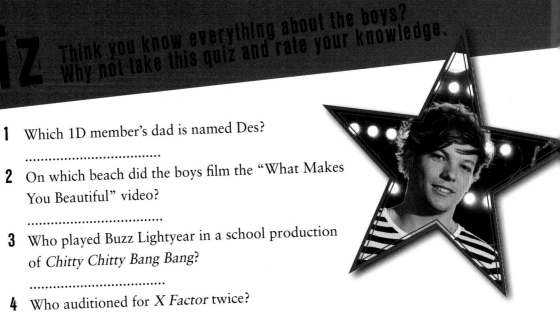

I ♥ ♪ 1D

1 Which 1D member's dad is named Des?

....

2 On which beach did the boys film the "What Makes You Beautiful" video?

....

3 Who played Buzz Lightyear in a school production of *Chitty Chitty Bang Bang*?

....

4 Who auditioned for *X Factor* twice?

....

5 Which 1D member was born on Christmas Eve?

....

6 Which 1D member doesn't have any sisters?

....

7 When 1D were greeted with hordes of screaming fans in the U.S., which legendary band were they compared to?

....

8 Who is the biggest Belieber in the band?

....

9 Which 1D member dated Rebecca Ferguson?

....